101 WACKY SPORTS QUOTES

by Jeff Parietti

illustrated by Don Orehek

No part of this publication may be reproduced in whole or in part, or stored in a retrieval system, or transmitted in any form or by any means, electronic, mechanical, photocopying, recording, or otherwise, without written permission of the publisher. For information regarding permission, write to Scholastic Inc., 730 Broadway, New York, NY 10003.

SCHOLASTIC INC.
New York Toronto London Auckland Sydney

*To my family —
especially my parents*

ISBN 0-590-44146-9

Copyright © 1991 by Jeff Parietti
Illustrations copyright © 1991 by Scholastic Inc.
All rights reserved. Published by Scholastic Inc.

12 11 10 9 8 7 6 5 4 3   5 6/9

Printed in the U.S.A.   01

First Scholastic printing, January 1991

SPORTS PUNS

Veteran New York Islanders hockey star Mike Bossy, dismissing a comment that his hair was going gray:

"That's a pigment of your imagination."

Boston Celtics forward Cedric "Cornbread" Maxwell on whether he knew about rookie Ken Bannister of the New York Knicks:

"The only Bannister I ever knew was the Star-Spangled Bannister."

Chicago White Sox outfielder Dave Gallagher, describing the play-by-play as a helicopter was circling above the diamond during a game:

"That's a high chopper over the mound."

New York Yankees designated hitter Ron Kittle, complaining about his meager salary:

"I'm so poor I can't even pay attention."

When an injured thumb caused San Diego Padres first baseman Steve Garvey to miss the last two months of the season, he handily came up with his motivation for the next season:

"I have just one goal: to be thumb-back player of the year."

New York Yankee Ron Swoboda,
after getting the call to pinch run
for designated hitter Jim Ray Hart
twice in a row:

*"Does that make me a Hart specialist?
Or the designated Hart transplant?"*

Comedian Alan King, commenting on the New York Giants' signing of placekicker Eddie Leopard:

"They'll probably use him only in spots."

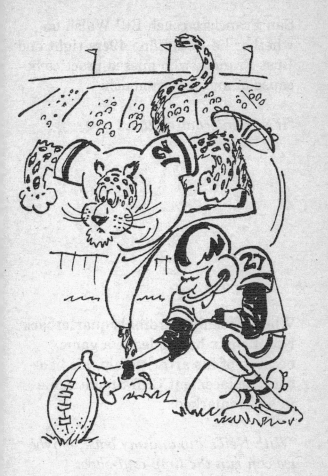

San Francisco coach Bill Walsh on whether he would fine 49ers tight end Russ Francis, who missed practice because of an upset stomach:

"It's an internal matter."

When Phoenix Cardinals quarterback Neil Lomax had to leave a game because of his arthritic hip, his bad-back replacement Cliff Stoudt came in and remarked:

"With Neil's hip and my back, maybe we can run the limp-and-shoot offense."

Atlanta owner Ted Turner, upon seeing Braves relief pitcher Jeff Dedmon sporting a plaid jacket:

"Dedmon, don't wear plaid."

Joe Torre, movie buff and California Angels radio announcer, on seeing infielder Glenn Hoffman get brushed back by a tight pitch:

"Is that called dustin' Hoffman?"

Radio broadcaster Scot Johnson, summing up a decisive football victory by the Humboldt State Lumberjacks over the Whittier College Poets:

"The ax is mightier than the pen."

Houston football coach Bill Yeoman, after the Cougars overcame a 21-point halftime deficit to tie Baylor in Waco, Texas, where a measles outbreak was occurring:

"I thought we had a rather spotty first-half performance."

Seattle Seahawks defensive end Jacob Green, trying to figure out the NFL's "half-sack" statistic:

"What's that — a Baggie?"

Ted Giannoulas, better known as the famous sports mascot "The Chicken," on whether hot weather made his fine-feathered costume unbearable to wear:

"If you can't stand the heat, stay out of The Chicken."

FRIENDLY INSULTS

Former San Diego Chargers quarterback Dan Fouts, becoming bold after retiring from pro football:

"Now that I'm retired, I want to say that all defensive backs are sissies."

Cincinnati Reds slugger George Foster, after learning that slow-footed, ungraceful outfielder Greg Luzinski of the Philadelphia Phillies had topped the National League by getting hit 10 times:

"Was that in the field or at the plate?"

Detroit forward John Sally, having some fun at the expense of Pistons teammate Mark Aquirre:

"We call Mark a lot of things 'cause his head's so big. Man, it's so big he has to go through a car wash to get it clean."

Professional golfer Lee Trevino on fellow pro J.C. Snead:

"He was so ugly as a kid his parents tied pork chops around his neck so that the dog would play with him."

College basketball announcer Al McGuire, explaining the intelligence level of football players:

"They do one-arm push-ups so that they can count with the other hand."

New York Ranger Chris Nilan on why he wasn't hurt by the head-butting tactics of Chicago Blackhawk Al Secord during a hockey brawl:

"He could have hurt me if there was anything more than air in his head."

Baseball announcer Joe Garagiola on how six-foot-three, 288-pound umpire Ken Kaiser keeps occupied after the season ends:

"In the off-season, he rents himself out as a handball court."

Cleveland Browns offensive tackle Doug Dieken, describing 14-year NFL defensive end Elvin Bethea of the Houston Oilers:

"Elvin is so old he had to use a jumper cable to get started last year."

Baseball announcer Bob Costas, putting into perspective just how old 45-year-old pitcher Tommy John of the New York Yankees really is:

"This guy is so old that the first time he had athlete's foot he used Absorbine Senior."

George Raveling, University of Southern California hoop coach, discussing basketball announcer Billy Packer's college days:

"Billy was recruited by Kentucky and North Carolina. Kentucky wanted him to go to North Carolina, and North Carolina wanted him to go to Kentucky."

Chicago Blackhawks broadcaster Dale Tallon — during a hockey game against the Winnipeg Jets — on the weather in Winnipeg:

"I wouldn't say it's cold, but every year Winnipeg's athlete of the year is an ice fisherman."

Los Angeles pitcher Don Sutton on the generosity of Dodgers manager Tommy Lasorda:

"Every year Tommy offers $50,000 to the family of the unknown soldier."

ANIMAL CRACKERS

Texas Rangers outfielder Mickey Rivers, commenting on the cold wind and 48-degree temperature at a game:

"It's so cold out there, I saw a dog chasing a cat, and they were both walking."

Detroit Lions coach Monte Clark, describing the beastly fear produced by tough NFL fullback Larry Csonka:

"When he goes on safari, the lions roll up their windows."

Minnesota manager Billy Gardner on just how rich Twins owner Carl Pohlad actually is:

"I hear he's so rich he bought his dog a boy."

Greyhound racetrack announcer
Duane Schlei, after a dog named
Little Itch was withdrawn before
the start of a race:

*"Ladies and gentlemen, please scratch
Little Itch."*

Thoroughbred trainer Herb Stevens, dismissing claims that a small horse he handled named Rockhill Native couldn't win the Kentucky Derby:

"If size meant anything, a cow could beat a rabbit."

Philadelphia Phillies relief pitcher Tug McGraw on the ups and downs of his game-saving duties:

"Some days you tame the tiger. And some days the tiger has you for lunch."

Atlanta Braves television announcer
Skip Caray on his introduction to
"The Chicken," the famous sports
mascot:

"Why did you cross the road?"

Pittsburgh outfielder Andy Van Slyke
on why it must be frustrating for Pirates manager Jim Leyland to guide
his last-place squad against the top
teams in the division horse race:

*"You can't ask Mr. Ed to keep up with
Secretariat."*

Los Angeles Raiders defensive end Howie Long, complaining that he was serving as the team decoy:

"I draw the attention, and the other guys make the plays. I should show up painted like a duck."

All-time hockey great Stan Mikita on why he didn't bother to consider a broadcasting career after hanging up his skates to end a 21-year career with the Chicago Blackhawks:

"Me on television is like putting earrings on a pig."

TRAINING TABLE

Upon hearing that beefy six-foot-five Pittsburgh outfielder Dave Parker had plans to become a vegetarian, Pirates teammate John Candelaria exclaimed:

"What are you going to eat? Redwoods?"

Ed Croke, public relations official for the New York Giants, on the results of the diet used by huge 295-pound defensive end Leonard Marshall:

"We put him on a Cambridge diet, and he ate half of Cambridge."

Boston coach Bill Fitch on hearing that rookie forward Kevin McHale was talking about playing basketball in Italy instead of signing with the Celtics:

"All I can say is, let him eat spaghetti."

Baseball announcer Bob Costas, describing the action as the television camera zeroed in for an up-close and personal shot of a fat male fan dressed as Batman:

"Holy calorie intake."

Boston Celtic Kevin McHale on whether his teammates would take in some culture during their exhibition-game trip to Spain:

"A lot of guys on this team think culture is going to McDonald's for lunch."

Portland Trail Blazers center Caldwell Jones, naming his favorite seafood:

"Saltwater taffy."

Jake LaMotta, one-time middleweight boxing champion, recalling one of the diets he tried in order to make the division weight:

"I tried this banana diet and didn't lose any weight, but you should have seen me climb trees."

Pittsburgh Pirates manager Jim Leyland, shaking his head at the fact that Chicago Cubs manager Don Zimmer does commercials for both a chicken dish and a diet plan:

"He's the only guy I know who gets paid to eat and diet."

Kansas City Royals trainer Mickey Cobb, who served as American League trainer for the All-Star Game in Montreal, on being able to order his meals in the French-speaking city without knowing the language:

"I didn't have any trouble ordering at restaurants. French toast for breakfast, French onion soup for lunch, French dip for dinner."

ALL IN THE FAMILY

Television broadcaster Tom Brookshier, after getting his first look at six-foot-four, 235-pound tight end Junior Miller of the Atlanta Falcons:

"I'd like to see Senior Miller."

As the mother of two speedy football sons, Raghib "Rocket" Ismail of Notre Dame and Quadri "Missile" Ismail of Syracuse, Fatima Ismail concluded that she also has a nickname:

"I guess I'm the launching pad."

New Jersey Nets guard Leon Wood on meeting the team's television broadcaster, Steve Albert:

"Are you any relation to your brother Marv?"

Pittsburgh Pirates shortstop Dale Berra, commenting on the comparisons some people make between him and his famous baseball father, Yogi:

"Our similarities are different."

Kathy Bosworth, mother of Seattle Seahawks linebacker Brian Bosworth, on the great deal of mischief "The Boz" got into during his childhood:

"It's a good thing Brian was a third child, or he would have been the only one."

Los Angeles Lakers center Swen Nater, who jokingly made up the names "Extermin Nater" and "Carmen Denomin Nater" to use in case he ever had kids, on another name his fertile imagination produced:

"The latest is Procrastin Nater."

San Francisco 49ers quarterback Joe Montana on whether he would encourage a son of his to play football and risk possible injury:

"Not if he can swing a golf club."

BONUS BABIES

The Citadel football coach Art Baker on his thoughts about six-foot-six, 310-pound offensive tackle Ronald Hale of upcoming opponent Vanderbilt:

"I wasn't that worried about him until I read in their press guide that he was born on November 1st, 15th, and 16th."

San Diego Padres manager Jack "Trader" McKeon on why his new infant granddaughter didn't have a name yet:

"She's the baby to be named later."

New Jersey Devils coach Tom McVie on how he had slept after a loss to the Buffalo Sabres:

"Oh, I slept like a baby. Every two hours I'd wake up and start crying."

Georgia State hoop coach Bob Reinhardt, describing his young team of eight freshmen, three sophomores, two juniors, and no seniors:

"We're so young we have to stop practices every few minutes to change diapers."

SPORTS SHORTS

Minnesota manager Billy Gardner, wondering about Twins outfielder Darrell "Downtown" Brown, who had homered just once in nearly 600 career at-bats:

"That must be an awful small town."

Southern Methodist University football coach Ron Meyer on the Mustangs' stocky five-foot-nine, 220-pound guard Harvey McAtee:

"He's so short his breath smells of earthworms."

Television basketball analyst Bucky Waters, after five-foot-five Kentucky guard Leroy Byrd was overmatched in the Wildcats' loss to the Alabama Crimson Tide:

"He's a great addition to your bench. He can sit on it, or under it."

IT'S ACADEMIC

Syracuse fullback Brent Ziegler on becoming the 265th selection in the National Football League draft:

"I think they drafted in alphabetical order."

Kansas City Royals relief hurler Steve Farr on why his having a sore pitching shoulder couldn't just all be in his head:

"How could it be mental? I don't have a college education."

Utah Jazz coach Frank Layden, recalling just how tough the students were at his Brooklyn, New York, high school:

"We had a lot of nicknames — Scarface, Blackie, Toothless — and those were just the cheerleaders."

San Diego State basketball coach David "Smokey" Gaines on his strong educational beliefs:

"I believe in higher education. You know, 6–8, 6–9, 6–10."

Kansas City Royals outfielder Willie Wilson, explaining the reason he refuses to sign autographs:

"When I was a little kid, teachers used to punish me by making me sign my name 100 times."

BRAINY QUIPS

Former NFL coach and star quarterback Norm Van Brocklin, describing the brain surgery he underwent:

"It was a brain transplant. I got a sportswriter's brain so I could be sure I had one that hadn't been used."

New York Mets junk ball pitcher Bob Ojeda on whether he would like to possess the blazing fastball of Mets reliever Randy Myers:

"Not if I have to have his brain, too."

Boston Celtics coach Bill Fitch, offering his thoughts on NBA referees:

"They have an impossible job, and they do an impossible job. If you put the brains of three officials into a hummingbird, it would still fly backward."

THE NUMBERS GAME

San Francisco television announcer Duane Kuiper after Giants lefty Dave Dravecky had thrown 66 pitches in six innings:

"It doesn't take a genius to figure out that's 12 per inning."

New Orleans Saints star running back George Rogers on his personal numerical goals for the football season:

"I want to gain 1,500 or 2,000 yards, whichever comes first."

Texas Rangers outfielder Mickey Rivers on his mathematical reason for being against an early-season baseball strike:

"There are more games in the second half than the first."

World Boxing Association welterweight champion Marlon Starling, on wanting to fight World Boxing Council welterweight champion Lloyd Honeyghan:

"I'll fight him for nothing if the price is right."

Pittsburgh Pirates catcher Junior Ortiz on whether his broken collarbone meant he would be out of action for six weeks:

"No, longer than that. Maybe a month and a half."

World middleweight wrist-wrestling champion Johnny Walker, analyzing his sport:

"It's about 90 percent strength and 40 percent technique."

Boxing promoter Don King, during a press conference for a bout between Mike Tyson and Tyrell Biggs:

"Mike Tyson has come 360 degrees around, and that's the triangle of life."

AMAZING TEAMWORK

Los Angeles Lakers superstar Magic
Johnson, expressing amazement at
how well he and teammate James
Worthy anticipate each other's moves
on the basketball court:

"It's almost like we have ESPN."

George Allen, television football analyst and ex-NFL coach, after Beasley
Reece of the New York Giants
downed a Green Bay Packers punt on
the one-yard line:

*"He made a great play. He kept his
body between himself and the ball."*

Southeast Missouri State basketball coach Ron Shumate, describing just how bad his team shot the ball during a game:

"It was so bad the players were giving each other high fives when they hit the rim."

Pro golfer Chi Chi Rodriguez on the advice his caddie offered him before he made a key pressure putt:

"He told me just to keep the ball low."

Boston Celtics forward M.L. Carr, recalling superstar Larry Bird's most amazing feat:

"Once we went out to eat, and he picked up the check."

Philadelphia 76ers forward Joe Bryant, denying that he's a selfish player:

"I just want to score my 25 points and help my teammates in every other way."

SEEING IS BELIEVING

After hitting a home run, Atlanta Braves hurler Tom Boggs was asked what type of pitch he had hit:

"I dunno; my eyes were closed."

New York Giants All-Pro linebacker Lawrence Taylor on running into Philadelphia Eagles quarterback Ron Jaworski at an off-season dinner:

"Gee, Ron, it's the first time I've seen you standing up."

Los Angeles Kings right wing Jim Fox, griping about the terrible condition of the ice at a local practice rink:

"I've seen better ice on my windshield."

AGONY OF DEFEAT

When seven-foot-four Virginia center Ralph Sampson dropped a throw to let the winning run score in a college softball contest, his basketball teammate Jeff Lamp exclaimed:

"Ralph probably feels about six-foot-nine right now."

When upset New York Rangers fans threw their free souvenirs onto the ice during the team's shutout loss to the Buffalo Sabres on Plastic Mug Night, Ranger rookie Tony Granato sighed in relief after the game:

"It's a good thing it wasn't Machete Night."

Stetson basketball coach Glenn Wilkes, moaning about his squad's tough schedule, which included several highly ranked opponents:

"We don't have a fight song; we have a surrender song."

Heavyweight boxer Riddick Bowe, describing the awesome punching power he packs against his opponents:

"Sometimes when I hit them with my right and knock 'em out, by the time they wake up, their clothes are out of style."

Longtime Princeton basketball coach Pete Carril, following a narrow 50—49 loss to No. 1-seeded Georgetown in the first round of the NCAA basketball tournament:

"I told my kids, as bad as you feel, feeling this bad is better than never getting a chance to feel this bad."

SPORTS HODGEPODGE

New York manager Yogi Berra, after the Yankees got speedy base-stealer Rickey Henderson in a trade:

"He can run anytime he wants. I'm giving him the red light."

U.S. volleyball team star Steve Timmons on whether teammates kidded him a lot because of his flattop haircut:

"No, but a couple of airplanes have tried to land on it."

Golfer Tom Watson on the reason he failed as a high school baseball player:

"I could only hit balls thrown down at my feet."

Former major league umpire Ron Luciano, confessing that he sometimes became confused while serving as home-plate umpire:

"I called a lot of 'baa-rikes' and 'stri-alls.'"

Johnny Kerr, basketball broadcaster and former NBA center, on how he would have guarded Kareem Abdul-Jabbar:

"I'd get real close to him and breathe on his goggles."

Philadelphia 76ers center Moses Malone on looking over his high hotel bill as he checked out:

"I only want to check out. I don't want to buy no hotel."

Former junior middleweight boxing champion Elisha Obed on which punch was his best:

"I don't know. I never hit myself."

Veteran golfer Lee Trevino on aging golfers:

"You know the first three things that go for a golfer? His nerves, his memory, and I can't remember the third."

Atlanta Falcons coach Jerry Glanville on one advantage of moving so many times during his long coaching career:

"I've got the kind of furniture that, when you snap your fingers, it jumps into the crate."

Northeastern Louisiana football coach Sam Goodwin on the difficulty he had getting his players used to air travel:

"We told them if they used chewing gum it would keep their ears from popping. It worked fine, except some of the guys had a hard time getting the gum out of their ears."

Bowler Don Carter on why he prefers his sport over golf:

"One of the advantages of bowling over golf is that you very seldom lose a bowling ball."

Los Angeles Raiders defensive back Lester Hayes, after trying to tackle slippery, scrambling quarterback Randall Cunningham of the Philadelphia Eagles:

"He must shower in Vaseline."

Race-car driver Janet Guthrie on why being a woman didn't prevent her from achieving success on the racetrack:

"You drive the car, you don't carry it."

Clemson middle guard William "The Refrigerator" Perry, after the NCAA banned the Tigers from appearing on television or in bowl games for two years:

"What makes it hard is that we can't watch television for two years."

New Jersey Nets center Darryl Dawkins, describing seven-foot-seven center Manute Bol of the Washington Bullets:

"He's so tall that if he fell down, he'd be halfway home."

Former major leaguer Bob Uecker —
now a baseball announcer and television star — on when he realized his
career with the Atlanta Braves was
finished:

*"When the manager, Luman Harris,
told me no visitors were allowed in the
clubhouse."*